Treasure House

Pupil Book 4
Comprehension

Author: Abigail Steel

William Collins' dream of knowledge for all began with the publication of his first book in 1819. A self-educated mill worker, he not only enriched millions of lives, but also founded a flourishing publishing house. Today, staying true to this spirit, Collins books are packed with inspiration, innovation and practical expertise. They place you at the centre of a world of possibility and give you exactly what you need to explore it.

Collins. Freedom to teach.

Published by Collins
An imprint of HarperCollins*Publishers*
The News Building
1 London Bridge Street
London
SE1 9GF

Browse the complete Collins catalogue at
www.collins.co.uk

© HarperCollins*Publishers* Limited 2015

10 9 8 7 6 5 4 3 2 1

ISBN 978-0-00-813345-0

The author asserts her moral right to be identified as the author of this work.

British Library Cataloguing in Publication Data
A Catalogue record for this publication is available from the British Library

Publishing Manager: Tom Guy
Project Managers: Dawn Booth and Kate Ellis
Edited by Hannah Hirst-Dunton
Cover design and artwork: Amparo Barrera
Internal design concept: Amparo Barrera
Typesetting: Jouve India Private Ltd
Illustrations: Eva Morales, Dante Ginevra, Andres Avery, Aptara and QBS

Printed in Italy by Grafica Veneta S.p.A.

Acknowledgements

The publishers wish to thank the following for permission to reproduce content. Every effort has been made to trace copyright holders and to obtain their permission for the use of copyright materials. The publishers will gladly receive any information enabling them to rectify any error or omission at the first opportunity.

HarperCollins Publishers Ltd for an extract from *Stowaway!* by Julian Jarman, copyright © 2007, Julian Jarman. Reproduced by permission of HarperCollins Publishers Ltd; David Higham Associates Ltd for the poem "I love our orange tent" by Berlie Doherty from *Story Chest: Big Bulgy Fat Black Slugs*, Thomas Nelson, 1993. Reproduced by permission of David Higham Associates Ltd; HarperCollins Publishers Ltd and David Higham Associates Ltd for an extract from *Cockadoodle-Doo, Mr Sultana!* by Michael Morpurgo and 1 illustration by Shoo Rayner, HarperCollins Children's Books, 2010, pp. 36–46, copyright © 2010, Michael Morpurgo and Shoo Rayner. Reproduced by permission of HarperCollins Publishers Ltd and David Higham Associates Ltd; Wes Magee for the poem "What is ... The Sun?" from *The Witch's Brew and Other Poems* by Wes Magee, Cambridge University Press, 1989. Reproduced by permission of the author Wes Magee; HarperCollins Publishers Ltd for an extract from *In the Rue Bel Tesoro* by Lin Coghlan, copyright © 2011, Lin Coghlan. Reproduced by permission of HarperCollins Publishers Ltd; Tunji Beier for the poem "Kob Antelope" translated by Ulli Beier. Reproduced by kind permission; and Andersen Press Ltd for an extract from *Angry Arthur* by Hiawyn Oram, 1982. Reproduced with permission.

(t = top, c = centre)

p. 4 (t) Gregar Rozac/Alamy, p. 4 (c) Martin Bennett/Alamy

Contents

Non-fiction (webpage): Thrills City

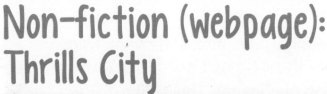

Home   About   Plan a visit   What's on   Our rides   Restaurants

Scariest rides ever:

The Brazen Beast   Techno Ride   Raging River's Revenge   Mighty Meteor   Vortex

An awesome day for all the family

- Escape on a once-in-a-lifetime adventure
- Unlimited fun all year round
- New this year – embark on an underwater adventure in the new sea-life aquarium
- Over the Rainbow Club – fab fun for our younger guests
- Live entertainment and characters
- Surprises at every turn
- Splash yourself silly in the water park!
- Stay overnight at our special 4 ★ family-friendly hotel
- Relax in our spa and health club

SPECIAL OFFERS

2-for-1 tickets before 13 July

Family Weekend Autumn Saver

Jump the queues and save 5% – print your tickets at home

OFFERS BY EMAIL

Sign up now to receive the latest information and offers and become a Select Guest

Title:
Surname:
Email:

Sign up

Open 10 a.m. to 6 p.m. every day ★ Close to motorway ★ Free parking

Get started

Copy these sentences carefully and complete them by filling in the gaps. Use the text from the webpage to find the answers.

1. Thrills City has a club for younger guests called the _____.

2. Guests might want to relax in the spa and _____.

3. You can have fun swimming in the _____.

4. If you sign up now for information and offers to be sent by email, you will become a _____.

5. You can watch live entertainment and meet _____.

Try these

Write a sentence to answer each question. One has been done for you.

1. Where would you click to learn more about events happening at Thrills City?

   Answer: *I would click on the 'What's on' button to learn more about events happening at Thrills City.*

2. How could you save money when buying tickets for a trip to Thrills City in June? Give both ways.

3. Could you visit the park on a Sunday? How do you know this?

4. Could you get something to eat there? Why do you think this?

5. What would be a good way to get there? Why do you think this?

Now try these

1. Imagine you are planning to visit Thrills City. What other information might you want to know? Write down your questions and make notes about where on this website you might find the answers.

2. Pretend you have clicked on the 'Plan a visit' button. Design the 'Plan a visit' webpage.

3. Think about how the information on this webpage might be presented if it were a leaflet rather than a webpage. Would the different webpages be different pages in the leaflet, or just different sections on a larger page? Would you add a map? When you have thought about this, design the leaflet.

Poetry: 'I Love Our Orange Tent'

I Love Our Orange Tent
by Berlie Doherty

I love our orange tent.
We plant it like a flower in the field.
The grass smells sweet inside it.
And at night
When we're lying in it,
I hear the owl crying.

When the wind blows,
my tent flaps
like a flying bird.

And the rain
patters down on it
with tiny footsteps.

I feel warm and safe
inside my tent.

But when the sun shines,
that's when I love it best!

When I wake up
and the sun is shining,
it pours in like yellow honey.
It glows like gold.
I love our orange tent.

Get started

Copy these sentences carefully and complete them by filling in the gaps. Use the poem to find the answers.

1. The poet sets up the tent in a _____.

2. At _____, she can hear an owl.

3. She can also hear the _____ dripping onto it.

4. She loves it best when _____.

5. The sun makes the tent _____ like gold.

Try these

Write a sentence to answer each question. One has been done for you.

1. What can the poet hear when she is in the tent?

   Answer: *When she is in the tent, the poet can hear an owl crying, the tent flapping and the rain pattering.*

2. Which other senses does the poet use to describe her experiences with the tent?

3. The words 'like a flower' are a simile. In your own words, explain what a simile is. Use a dictionary to help you if necessary.

4. Write down the three other similes in the poem.

5. Does the poet go camping on her own? Why do you think this?

Now try these

1. Why do you think the line 'I love our orange tent' is repeated at the beginning and the end of the poem? What effect does the repetition have on you as a reader?

2. Imagine you are the poet, camping in the orange tent. Write a short diary entry about what you can see, hear, smell and feel. Your diary entry should contain some new ideas. It should not be a poem.

3. Think about something you love doing. Use four similes of your own to describe what it is like.

Poetry: 'The Donkey'

'The Donkey' by Anon.

I saw a donkey
One day old,
His head was too big
For his neck to hold;
His legs were shaky
And long and loose,
They rocked and staggered
And weren't much use.

He tried to gambol
And frisk a bit,
But he wasn't quite sure
Of the trick of it.
His queer little coat
Was soft and grey,
And curled at his neck
In a lovely way.

His face was wistful
And left no doubt
That he felt life needed
Some thinking about.
So he blundered round
In venturesome quest,
And then lay flat
On the ground to rest.

He looked so little
And weak and slim,
I prayed the world
Might be good to him.

Get started

Copy these sentences and complete them by filling in the gaps. Use the poem to find the answers.

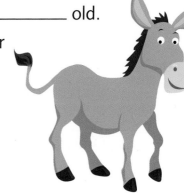

1. The donkey was _____ _____ old.

2. His _____ seemed too small for his _____.

3. He had a soft, grey _____.

4. The poet thought the donkey's face looked _____.

5. Eventually, the donkey lay down to _____ on the ground.

Try these

Write a sentence to answer each question. One has been done for you.

1. Why couldn't the donkey move around well?

   Answer: *The donkey couldn't move around well because it was very young and just learning to walk.*

2. Explain the meanings of the words 'gambol', 'frisk', 'blundered', 'venturesome' and 'quest'. Use a dictionary for help if necessary.

3. What do the words you explained make you think about the donkey's attitude?

4. How do you think the poet felt about the donkey? Why do you think this?

5. Why do you think the poet 'prayed the world might be good to him'?

Now try these

1. The poet believes that the donkey 'felt life needed some thinking about'. Imagine the donkey can put these thoughts into words. Note down some questions he might like to ask and ideas about what he might hope to do next.

2. Find the seven pairs of rhyming words. Look at how the rhymes are arranged. Then write one new verse about the donkey using the same arrangement of rhymes.

3. Draw a picture of the donkey trying to gambol. Use the poem to help you make your drawing detailed.

Non-fiction (newspaper report): The Accident

LATEST NEWS

SECOND ICE FATALITY IN A WEEK

Tragedy struck again yesterday when an elderly lady fell through the ice. Mrs Wills, of Onslow Gardens, had been walking alone with her sister's dog when it chased a duck onto the frozen river. It is the first time in living memory that the River Thames has frozen from bank to bank.

Onlookers struggled desperately to save Mrs Wills, 79, when she fell through the ice whilst trying to rescue the black Labrador.

Rescue services were on the scene within five minutes, but as Chief Officer Chung said, "There was no way anyone could survive more than a minute or two in water with sub-zero temperatures." Last week, the same rescue crew tried unsuccessfully to rescue an eight-year-old boy who had been playing on the ice.

Get started

Copy these sentences carefully and complete them by filling in the gaps. Use the newspaper report to find the answers.

1. Yesterday, an elderly lady fell through the _____ .

2. The River _____ had frozen over.

3. Mrs Wills lived in _____ _____ .

4. Mrs Wills was _____ years old.

5. The dog was a black _____ .

Try these

Write a sentence to answer each question. One has been done for you.

1. When was the last time someone remembered the River Thames freezing from bank to bank?

   Answer: *Never, as this was the first time in living memory that the River Thames had frozen from bank to bank.*

2. With whom had Mrs Wills been walking?

3. The rescue crew arrived very quickly. Why didn't Mrs Wills survive?

4. Why do you think Mrs Wills went onto the ice?

5. Do you think it would be safe to play on the frozen Thames? Why do you think this?

Now try these

1. Imagine a news reporter interviewed someone who saw the accident. Write at least three sentences as though this person is saying them, describing what they saw.

2. Write two extra paragraphs for the newspaper report. One could contain the interview with the person who saw the accident. One could add extra information: did the rescue crew save the dog? Use dramatic language and clear descriptions to match the style of the newspaper report.

3. Design a poster that could be displayed to warn people of the dangers of frozen rivers. What might people need to know? Use some of the information from the newspaper report to help you.

Non-fiction (diary): Holiday diary

Holiday diary

Friday 2 August

Bored, bored, bored! This is our holiday, so you'd think it would be fun. Huh! Raj just sits playing games on his phone all day – he might as well not be on holiday at all, because he doesn't seem to want to go out or play or do anything interesting. Mum and Dad are so exhausted (apparently) that all they really want to do is flop. Still, they've promised to take me to the beach this afternoon. Maybe there'll be someone to play with there.

Later …

The beach was brilliant! It's really wide, flat and sandy. The sand is excellent for running on, and also for digging and making sandcastles. I had a great time, but you'll never guess what the best thing was. I made friends with this really nice girl, Stacey. She's coming over to our holiday house tomorrow to play.

Saturday 3 August

Today was just … amazing. I'm still trying to work out how I feel about it actually. Stacey came over, and we were playing a great game in the garden of the holiday house, when we noticed a little plane flying overhead. It seemed to be flying a bit low, but we didn't really think about it – until we suddenly saw clouds of smoke billowing out of the back of it! Then, suddenly, it dropped down into the sea. The pilot of the plane must have pressed the 'eject' button because we could see him floating down by parachute. Stacey and I just stared at each other. We were in shock. Then Stacey realised we had to phone for help.

"Meena!" she said. "Grab the phone and dial 999. We need Air-Sea Rescue!" I quickly got on the phone, and told the lady where we were and what we had seen. The lady said they would send a helicopter at once. Sure enough, within minutes we saw a big orange helicopter hovering over the sea where the plane had crashed. A rescue worker was lowered down on a rope, and grabbed the pilot of the plane, who was clinging to the wreckage. Then the pair of them got winched up into the helicopter and flew away.

I hope the pilot is OK. Mum says Stacey and I probably saved his life.

Get started

Copy these sentences and complete them by filling in the gaps. Use the diary entry to find the answers.

1. The girl writing the diary is called _____.

2. Her mum and dad felt _____ on Friday.

3. Raj didn't want to do _____ interesting.

4. The two girls met on _____ afternoon.

5. Stacey went to Meena's holiday house on _____.

Try these

Write a sentence to answer each question. One has been done for you.

1. How did the girls know the pilot ejected?

   Answer: *The girls knew the pilot ejected because they could see him floating down by parachute.*

2. Who arrived to help the pilot?

3. Who do you think Raj is? Why do you think this?

4. How do you think Meena will feel about what happened on Saturday when she works it out?

5. How do you think Meena's mum feels about what happened? Why do you think this?

Now try these

1. How do you think Stacey feels about what happened since she met Meena? Write at least three sentences as though Stacey is saying them.

2. Write Meena's diary entry for the next day. What might she and Stacey do? Is Raj more interested in joining in? Remember to use diary features.

3. Imagine you are Meena or Stacey, and that Air-Sea Rescue has asked you to draw a picture of what you saw. Make sure all the details from the extract are in the picture.

Fiction (fable): 'The Eagle and the Turtle'

'The Eagle and the Turtle' – a fable by Aesop

The Turtle was not satisfied with his life. He wanted to stop being a turtle.

"I'm tired of swimming about in the sea and crawling about on the beach, getting nowhere in particular," he grumbled. "I want to be able to fly in the air like an eagle."

He spoke to the Eagle about it.

"You're not built for flying," the Eagle told the Turtle. "You haven't any wings."

"Don't worry about that," answered the Turtle. "I've watched how the birds do it. I've watched them soar and glide, skim and dive. Even if I haven't got wings, I can make my four flippers act like four stout oars in the air, the way I do in the water. Just get me up there, and you'll see I can fly as well as any of the birds – probably better! Besides, if you'll carry me as high as the clouds, I'll bring you lots of rare pearls from the sea."

The Eagle was tempted, and carried the Turtle up to a great height.

"Now, then!" cried the Eagle. "Fly!"

But the moment the Turtle was on his own, he fell from the sky. He fell like a stone, and on a stone he landed. He struck with such force that he smashed into little pieces.

Moral: Be satisfied with what you are.

Get started

Copy these sentences carefully and complete them by filling in the gaps. Use the fable to find the answers.

1. The Turtle was not _____ with being a turtle.

2. He was _____ of swimming about in the sea.

3. He decided to speak to the _____ about his problem.

4. The Eagle told the Turtle he wasn't _____ for flying.

5. But the Turtle insisted the Eagle carry him as high as the _____.

Try these

Write a sentence to answer each question. One has been done for you.

1. Why was the Turtle unhappy with his life?

   Answer: *The Turtle was unhappy with his life because he was tired of getting nowhere in particular.*

2. Which part of his body did the Turtle think would be as good as wings?

3. In your own words, explain the moral of the story.

4. Why do you think the Eagle agreed to carry the Turtle into the clouds?

5. What do you think the Eagle expected to happen? Why do you think this?

Now try these

1. What might the Eagle really think of the Turtle? Write three sentences as though the Eagle is saying them.

2. Rewrite the extract from the Eagle's point of view. What parts of the story will change?

3. Draw a picture of the Turtle talking to the Eagle. Add thought bubbles to show what they are each thinking.

Fiction (classic): 'Cockadoodle-Doo, Mr Sultana!'

From 'Cockadoodle-Doo, Mr Sultana!' by Michael Morpurgo

Out in the countryside, the little red rooster was scratching around in the dusty farm track at the edge of the cornfield.

He scratched and he scratched. Suddenly there was something strange in the earth, something different, something very pretty that glistened and shone and twinkled in the sun. He tried eating it, but it didn't taste very good. So he dropped it. And then he had a sudden and brilliant idea.

"I know," he said to himself. "Poor old mistress mine loves pretty things. She's always saying so, and she's got nothing pretty of her own. I'll take it home for her. Then she won't be cross with me for running away, will she?"

But just as he picked it up again, along the farm track came the great fat Sultan on his horse, and in front of him, dozens of his servants, all of them crawling on their hands and knees in the dirt.

Closer and closer they came. All at once they spotted the little red rooster **and** the diamond button too, glinting in his beak.

"There my lord Sultan!" they cried. "LOOK! That little red rooster. He's got your diamond button."

"So that's what it is," the little red rooster said to himself.

The great fat Sultan rode up, scattering his servants hither and thither as he came. "Little Red Rooster," he said from high up on his horse. "I see you have my diamond button.

I am your great and mighty Sultan. Give it to me at once. It's valuable, very valuable. And it's **mine**."

"I don't think so, Mr Sultana," replied the little red rooster, who had never in his life been frightened of anyone or anything. "COCKADOODLE-DOO, Mr Sultana. Finders keepers. If it's so valuable, then I'm going to give it to poor mistress mine. She needs it a lot more than you, I think. Sorry, Mr Sultana."

"**What**!" spluttered the Sultan. "Mr Sultana? How dare you speak to me like that? How dare you? Did you hear what that infernal bird called me? Fetch me that rooster. Fetch me my diamond button! Grab him! Grab that rooster!"

There was a frightful kerfuffle of dust and feathers … and SQUAWKING, as the Sultan's servants tried to grab the little red rooster. Whatever they did, they just could not catch him. In the end, the little red rooster ran off into the cornfield. But although he'd escaped their clutches, he was very cross with himself, for in all the kerfuffle he had dropped the diamond button.

Get started

Copy these sentences carefully and complete them by filling in the gaps. Use the story to find the answers.

1. The main character of this story is the little _____.

2. He found something shiny on the dusty _____ _____ by the cornfield.

3. The shiny item was a _____ _____.

4. The button belonged to the _____.

5. The rooster ran away into the _____, but he dropped the button!

Try these

Write a sentence to answer each question. One has been done for you.

1. Why did the Sultan want the button back?

Answer: *The Sultan wanted the button back because it was very valuable.*

2. What is a 'sultan'? What is a 'sultana'? Use a dictionary for help if necessary. What do you think a 'kerfuffle' is?

3. Find three reasons the little red rooster wanted to give the item to his mistress.

4. How do you think the little red rooster felt when he was asked to give the button back?

5. Do you think the Sultan expected this response? Why do you think this?

Now try these

1. How do you think the Sultan feels now? Write three sentences as though the Sultan is saying them.

2. Write a different ending, where the rooster doesn't lose the button. What do you think the rooster's mistress would do if he took it to her?

3. Draw a picture of the confrontation between the Sultan and the little red rooster. Use speech bubbles to show what they are saying to each other. Add some thought bubbles to show what the Sultan's servants think.

Fiction (classic): 'The Wind in the Willows'

From 'The Wind in the Willows' by Kenneth Grahame

The Mole, who had been busily spring-cleaning his house, had come out for a rest.

As he sat on the grass and looked across the river, a dark hole in the bank opposite, just above the water's edge, caught his eye. Something bright and small seemed to twinkle down in the heart of it, vanish, then twinkle once more like a tiny star. But it could hardly be a star in such an unlikely situation, and it was too glittering and too small for a glow-worm. Then, as he looked, it winked at him, and so declared itself to be an eye, and a small face began gradually to grow up round it, like a frame round a picture. A brown little face, with whiskers.

A grave round face, with the same twinkle in its eye that had first attracted his notice. Small neat ears and thick silky hair. It was the Water Rat!

The Rat said nothing, but stooped and unfastened a rope and hauled on it, then lightly stepped into a little boat which the Mole had not observed. It was painted blue outside and white within, and was just the size for two animals, and the Mole's whole heart went out to it at once, even though he did not yet fully understand its uses.

The Rat sculled smartly across and made fast. Then he held up his fore-paw as the Mole stepped gingerly down. "Lean on that!" he said. "Now then, step lively!" and the Mole to his surprise and rapture found himself actually seated in the stern of a real boat.

"This has been a wonderful day!" he said, as the Rat shoved off and took to the sculls again. "Do you know, I've never been in a boat before in all my life."

Get started

Copy these sentences carefully and complete them by filling in the gaps. Use the story to find the answers.

1. The Mole had needed a rest from _____-_____ his house.

2. He was sitting on the grass next to the _____.

3. The Water Rat had silky hair and small neat _____.

4. The boat was just the size for _____ _____.

5. The Mole had _____ been in a boat before.

Try these

Write a sentence to answer each question. One has been done for you.

1. Why couldn't the Mole see the Water Rat's eye properly at first?

Answer: *The Mole couldn't see the Water Rat's eye properly at first because the Water Rat was in a dark hole.*

2. What do the words 'stooped', 'hauled', 'sculled' and 'rapture' mean? Use a dictionary for help if necessary.

3. How did the Mole feel about being in the boat?

4. Did the Mole expect the Water Rat to invite him onto the boat? How do you know?

5. Do you think the Mole and the Water Rat already knew each other? Why do you think that?

Now try these

1. What might the Water Rat have thought about the Mole at first? Write three sentences as though the Water Rat is thinking them.

2. Rewrite the extract from the Water Rat's point of view.

3. Draw a detailed picture of the Water Rat sculling towards the Mole.

Fiction (historical): 'Stowaway!'

This historical adventure tells the story of a young Tudor boy in the sixteenth century, and his dream to sail with the famous Captain Francis Drake.

From 'Stowaway!' by Julia Jarman

How Dickon envied his best friend, Tib, who was aboard the 'Pelican', for the famous Francis Drake was its Captain – Francis Drake, England's greatest sailor and friend of Good Queen Bess. Francis Drake who had come back from the Spanish Main, his ship laden with gold. And now he was setting out on another exciting voyage – with Tib as his cabin boy.

Dickon gritted his teeth to stop the tears. He'd tried to get a job, but the second mate had taken one look at his lame leg and said, "Sorry, lad. We only take the fit and able. You couldn't climb the mainmast."

"I could …" But the second mate hadn't listened. Instead, he said to Tib, "You'll do. You look a strong lad." So Tib would have gold for his mother when the ship returned to Plymouth. Dickon would have nothing, and his poor widowed mother had eight boys to feed.

Dickon was suddenly jolted out of his misery by a loud voice. "Here, boy, carry this!" A young gentleman in a leather doublet had dropped a bag at Dickon's feet.

Then a gentleman with dark hair and beard called out from the 'Pelican'.

"Cousin John! Not a moment too soon. We sail at five!" Dickon couldn't believe his eyes. It was Francis Drake! It must be. He wore a gold chain round his neck.

"Cousin Francis!" The young gentleman ran up the gangway. Dickon ran after him, carrying the bag. He could run and climb. He could do lots of things.

Get started

Copy these sentences and complete them by filling in the gaps. Use the story to find the answers.

1. _____ and _____ were best friends.

2. Francis Drake was the _____ of the 'Pelican'.

3. Tib was Drake's _____ boy.

4. Dickon had a _____ leg.

5. Despite his leg, Dickon knew he could _____ and _____.

Try these

Write a sentence to answer each question. One has been done for you.

1. Why did the second mate say Dickon couldn't do the job?

   Answer: *The second mate said that Dickon couldn't do the job because Dickon had a lame leg and wouldn't be able to climb the mainmast.*

2. What do the words 'doublet', 'lame' and 'widowed' mean? Use a dictionary for help if necessary. What do the words 'lame' and 'widowed' tell you about the life of Dickon and his family?

3. Who was the man who threw Dickon the bag?

4. What did this man want Dickon to do?

5. Find three pieces of evidence in the text that show it is a historical story.

Now try these

1. What do you think Dickon will want to know about the ship and the voyage? Write three questions as though Dickon is asking them.

2. Write a diary entry as though Tib is writing it. How do you think Tib feels about the voyage? How did he feel when he thought Dickon would be left behind?

3. Draw a detailed picture of Dickon. Choose whether you will draw him when he thinks he will be left behind, or when he is running with John's bag. Use the extract to help you.

Playscript: 'In the Rue Bel Tesoro'

This is the beginning of a play about children living in a country where soldiers are fighting and people are struggling to survive.

From 'In the Rue Bel Tesoro' by Lin Coghlan

SCENE 1

(A busy train station crowded with travellers. Sasha and Omar arrive pushing an old-fashioned pram and carrying a bag stuffed with belongings.)

SASHA: Don't say anything, Omar; let me do the talking.

OMAR: (into the pram) You've got to keep quiet, Valentine, we're in the station now.

(They approach a soldier checking documents at the entrance to the platform.)

SOLDIER: Papers?

SASHA: (handing over the papers) We're going to meet our mother. She's waiting for us.

SOLDIER: The baby – his pass?

SASHA: He's … a new baby, he doesn't have one.

SOLDIER: No papers, I can't let you through.

(Fran arrives with a huge suitcase and pushes in.)

FRAN: Please – let an old woman by! My bad hip! My feet!

SOLDIER: (unmoved) Papers?

(Fran gives him her papers as the children watch.)

SOLDIER: Go through.

(Fran hurries through the barrier. Sasha grabs Omar and drags him after Fran, getting away from the soldier.)

SOLDIER: Hey, you! Come back!

(Sasha and Omar disappear into the crowd.)

SCENE 2

(Fran staggers into the train compartment with her bundles.)

SASHA: Please, madam, if we could stay with you, we're on our own …

FRAN: Oh no – impossible. I must have my space.

SASHA: The soldiers don't stop old people so much when they have children.

FRAN: I don't like babies.

OMAR: It isn't a baby – it's a dog.

(Sasha looks at him furiously.)

Get started

Copy these sentences carefully and complete them by filling in the gaps. Use the playscript to find the answers.

1. Scene 1 is set in a busy _____ _____.

2. Sasha and Omar's bag is stuffed with _____.

3. The soldier checks everyone's _____.

4. Fran is an _____ _____.

5. Omar tells Fran they have a _____, not a _____.

Try these

Write a sentence to answer each question. One has been done for you.

1. Where is Valentine?

   Answer: *Valentine is in the pram.*

2. Why does Sasha want to stay with Fran?

3. Why is Sasha furious with Omar?

4. How do you think the children feel? Why might they feel like this?

5. Look at the text from the extract that is in brackets. What does this text tell you?

Now try these

1. What do you know about the place where the children are? What would you like to find out in order to understand the play better? Write notes about the information you already have and the information you would like to have.

2. Write a short message from Sasha to her mother, telling her about what happened at the train station. Try to imagine what events and feelings Sasha might want to write about.

3. Rewrite Scene 2 as a chapter from a story instead of a playscript. How will you explain and describe what is happening?

Fiction: 'The Day the Helicopters Came'

This story is about how frightening it was for a child when an army invaded a village during the Vietnam War in the 1960s.

'The Day the Helicopters Came' by Rachel Anderson

We had a cow for milk, some hens, and a goat. We harvested enough rice and vegetables for our family and the rest my mother sent downriver to market in the city.

Then one day the helicopters came. We watched them circle, then bump down, one after another in rapid succession, onto our vegetable gardens. The men jumped out and ran, bent double as though themselves afraid of being fired on, over melons, beans, celery, trampling with their boots on whatever produce hadn't already been destroyed by shells. "We must go in," said my mother, and she hurried us inside. But my grandmother was in a trance, dazed by three nights in the shelter. My mother sat her down gently on the stool and gave her the baby to hold while she saw to the clearing up.

The room was suddenly darkened by a huge man, higher than the door lintel, blocking out the light. He was so tall that he had to stoop to stand in the doorway, and even then the top of his helmet was lost in the grass thatch.

"Where's your husband, lady?" he shouted. My mother snatched the baby back from my grandmother and held it to her tightly. The man instinctively twitched his gun back at her. He was very frightened.

"Your husband! Where is he?"

He didn't see me. I was in the folds of my father's jacket hanging on a peg. But as I flattened myself more against the wall I knocked an earthenware dish down from the shelf. It clattered to the floor.

Get started

Copy these sentences carefully and complete them by filling in the gaps. Use the story to find the answers.

1. The girl's family had a cow because it could give them _____.

2. Her mother sent their spare rice and vegetables to the _____ in the _____.

3. The helicopters landed on the _____ _____.

4. The men jumped out and _____.

5. The girl's mother _____ the family inside.

Try these

Write a sentence to answer each question. One has been done for you.

1. Why was the girl's grandmother 'in a trance'?

   Answer: *The girl's grandmother was 'in a trance' because she had spent three nights in the shelter.*

2. What do the words 'succession' and 'lintel' mean? In the setting of the extract, what are 'shells'? Use a dictionary for help if necessary.

3. How do you think the soldiers felt as they ran from the helicopter? Why do you think this?

4. The girl says the soldier in the doorway was very frightened. How do you think she knew this?

5. Why do you think the soldiers trampled on the vegetables?

Now try these

1. How might the girl's grandmother feel about what is happening? Write at least three sentences as though she is saying them.

2. Write at least eight lines of dialogue that might occur next between the girl's mother and the soldier in the doorway. What would they ask each other? Remember to think about how they might feel.

3. Draw a detailed picture of the soldiers running in the vegetable patch. Add a caption to your picture, as though it will be used in a newspaper report.

Poetry: Humans – Friends or Foes?

Look carefully at this Ragamala painting from medieval India, and read this poem by an unknown Nigerian poet. Both are about the relationship between people and animals.

'Kob Antelope' by Anon. (Yoroba), an unknown Nigerian poet

A creature to pet and
spoil like a child.
Smooth-skinned
stepping cautiously
in the lemon grass …
The eyes
like a bird's.
The head
beautiful like carved wood …
Your neck seems long,
so very long
to the greedy hunter.

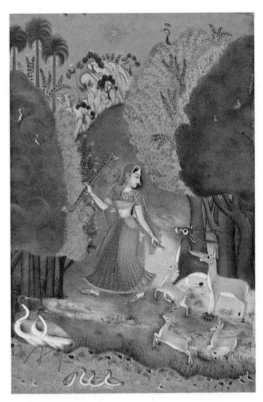

Todi Ragini
A Ragamala painting

Get started

Copy these sentences carefully and complete them by filling in the gaps. Use the poem and the painting to find the answers.

1. The poem is about a kob _____.

2. There are four deer and one _____ in the painting.

3. The painting is from _____ and the poem is from _____.

4. The animal in the poem has _____ skin.

5. The animal in the poem has a _____ neck.

Try these

Write a sentence to answer each question. One has been done for you.

1. Who is the other character mentioned in the poem?

   Answer: *The hunter is the other character mentioned in the poem.*

2. In your own words, explain the way the antelope moves. Use a dictionary for help if necessary.

3. Why do you think the hunter is interested in the antelope? Explain your answer.

4. How do you think the poet feels about the antelope? Why do you think this?

5. Look at the painting. How do you think the woman and the deer feel about each other? Why do you think this?

Now try these

1. Find three similes in the poem that describe what the antelope is like. Then think about what the deer in the painting are like. Write down at least three similes to describe the deer in the painting.

2. Imagine you are the woman in the painting. Write a poem like 'Kob Antelope' about the deer. Think carefully about your descriptions and what might happen in the forest. Use at least one new simile.

3. Draw a picture of the antelope in a forest. Use ideas from the poem and from the painting. Will you show the hunter? Will you show the poet?

Fiction: 'Angry Arthur' and Poetry: 'My Hair as Black as Dirty Coal'

Here are two pieces of writing about being angry: one is prose and one is poetry. In 'Angry Arthur', not being allowed to watch his favourite TV programme makes Arthur very, very angry. Bertie Thomson won a prize for his poem about anger when he was nine years old.

From 'Angry Arthur' by Hiawyn Oram

"No," said his mother, "it's too late. Go to bed."

"I'll get angry," said Arthur.

"Get angry," said his mother.

So he did. Very, very angry.

He got so angry that his anger became a stormcloud exploding thunder and lightning and hailstones.

"That's enough," said his mother. But it wasn't.

Arthur's anger became a hurricane hurling rooftops and chimneys and church spires.

"That's enough," said his father. But it wasn't.

Arthur's anger became a typhoon tipping whole towns into the sea.

"That's enough," said his grandfather. But it wasn't.

Arthur's anger became a universequake and the earth and the moon and the stars and the planets, Arthur's country and Arthur's town, his street, his house, his garden and his bedroom were nothing more than bits in space.

Arthur sat on a bit of Mars and thought. He thought and thought. "Why was I so angry?" he thought. He never did remember. Can you?

'My Hair as Black as Dirty Coal' by Bertie Thomson

My hair as black as dirty coal,
My eyes sizzle like fried eggs in a pan,
My nose breathes heavily like a charging wild bull.
Because:

(My brother ...)

My mouth breathing fire like a dragon.
My stomach going in and out,
I clench my fists hard like compressing a lemon
Until all the juice comes out.

(kicked my ...)

My anger bubbling inside,
Ready to fire out of my head.
I think I'm Arnold
Schwarzenegger.
My feet heat up ready to kick out
And then I burst out.

(ball over the fence!!)

Get started

Copy these sentences carefully and complete them by filling in the gaps. Use the story and the poem to find the answers.

1. Arthur's anger first became a _____ exploding thunder.

2. It then hurled rooftops and _____ and _____ _____.

3. Arthur was angry because his mother said he couldn't watch a _____ _____.

4. The poet was breathing like a _____ _____ bull.

Try these

Write a sentence to answer each question. One has been done for you.

1. How are the two extracts similar?

   Answer: *The two extracts are similar because they are both about anger.*

2. What is the effect of the words in brackets in the poem?

3. Find four similes in the poem.

4. The words 'his anger became a stormcloud' are a metaphor. In your own words, explain what a metaphor is. Use a dictionary for help.

5. What are hurricanes and typhoons? Use a dictionary for help if necessary. What do you think a 'universequake' is? Explain how these words help you to imagine Arthur's anger.

Now try these

1. Why do you think these writers use similes and metaphors? What effect do they have on you as a reader?

2. How do you think the poet's brother feels? Write down at least three ideas for similes that explain how he might be feeling.

3. Imagine feeling very happy. Write a paragraph that uses metaphors to show what your happiness is like. If you need to, use the 'Angry Arthur' story for ideas about how to write your metaphors.

Non-fiction (information text): Feathered record breakers

Feathered record breakers

Biggest alive

The giant of the bird world is the ostrich, from Africa. It grows up to 2.7 metres and can weigh over 155 kilograms. Its eggs are also the biggest, weighing in at 1.5 kilograms.

Heaviest extinct bird

The roc, or elephant bird, lived in Madagascar until 300 years ago. It weighed over 420 kilograms, and laid eggs seven times as big as the ostrich.

Heaviest flier

The African Kori bustard has been known to weigh 18 kilograms.

Tallest extinct bird

Some species of the New Zealand moa grew to over 4 metres, but they died out about 700 years ago.

Fastest flier

Spine-tailed swifts can reach 170 kilometres per hour.

Fastest runner

Ostriches can run at 65 kilometres per hour.

Greatest wingspan

The wandering albatross has a wingspan up to 3 metres.

Smallest bird

The bee hummingbird measures less than 6 centimetres from beak to tail and weighs 2 grams.

Deepest divers

Emperor penguins have been known to reach depths of over 250 metres.

Get started

Copy these sentences carefully and complete them by filling in the gaps. Use the facts to find the answers.

1. The fastest flier is the _____-_____ _____.

2. Emperor penguins have dived over _____ _____ deep.

3. The biggest bird alive is the _____.

4. A bee hummingbird weighs only _____ _____.

5. The roc weighed over _____ _____.

Try these

Write a sentence to answer each question. Use the text to help you. One has been done for you.

1. Which bird holds two of these records? Which records does it hold?

   Answer: *The ostrich holds two of these records: the biggest bird alive and the fastest runner.*

2. What does 'wingspan' mean? Use a dictionary for help if necessary. Which of the birds in the extract do you think has the smallest wingspan?

3. Do the facts tell you whether the ostrich or the roc was taller? If so, which was taller?

4. Why do you think the author included birds that are extinct?

5. Why do you think this text uses subheadings?

Now try these

1. In your own words, write three different facts about birds. If you can, discover interesting new facts by doing some research.

2. Which feathered record breaker do you think is the most interesting? Write a paragraph to tell someone else about this bird, explaining why you think it is the most interesting.

3. Draw a picture of an ostrich with its eggs. Label it with information boxes, using the details given in the text.

Non-fiction (information text): What is the Sun? and Poetry: 'What is the Sun?'

In this unit we explore two different ways of describing the Sun – in a non-fiction text and in a poem.

What is the Sun?

The Sun is a star. It is the nearest star to Earth, which is why it seems much bigger than any other star, but really the Sun is quite a small star. Some stars that are much further away are thousands of times bigger than the Sun.

The Sun is a huge ball of fiery gas. It is 150 million kilometres from Earth, and without it there would be no light or warmth on Earth. If the Sun did not give us light and heat there would be no life on Earth, so the Sun is very important to us. We are not its only planet, though; it has eight others.

It takes about 365 days, or one year, to travel once around the Sun.

'What is the Sun?' by Wes Magee

The Sun is an orange dinghy
sailing across a calm sea.

It is a gold coin
dropped down a drain in heaven.

It is a yellow beach ball
kicked high into the summer sky.

It is a red thumb-print
on a sheet of pale blue paper.

It is the gold top from a milk bottle
floating on a puddle.

Get started

Copy these sentences carefully and complete them by filling in the gaps. Use the facts and the poem to find the answers.

1. The Sun is the nearest star to _____.

2. The Sun is quite a _____ star.

3. Without the Sun we would have no
   _____ or _____.

4. According to the poem, the sun is a yellow
   _____ _____.

5. According to the poem, the sky is like a
   sheet of _____ _____ _____.

Try these

Write a sentence to answer each question. One has been done for you.

1. Why is the Sun important to us?

   Answer: *The Sun is important to us because there would be no light, warmth or life on Earth without it.*

2. How many metaphors are there in the poem? How many metaphors are there in the non-fiction text?

3. The non-fiction text says the Sun is made of gas, but the poem suggests the Sun is made of gold. Is the Sun made of gas or gold? Why do you think this?

4. How does the poem describe the Sun differently from the non-fiction text?

5. Do either of the texts tell you exactly how hot the Sun is? Which one do you think would be most likely to tell you? Why do you think this?

Now try these

1. Why does the poem describe the Sun differently from the non-fiction text? Write notes about what each writer was trying to do.

2. Explain which description of the Sun you prefer and why. Which way would you choose to describe the Sun to someone who didn't know what it was? Why would you choose this?

3. Draw two pictures of the Sun. Include Earth in one, and use the details from the non-fiction text to add information boxes. Use ideas from the poem to draw the second picture.